GET HIRED

by Brian Harris, B.A., M. Ed.

**Learn six employer secrets
that can improve your cover letter,
resume, networking skills, and
job interview results to help you gain
employment in a new career**

CGS COMMUNICATIONS, INC.

www.millionairelifeguard.com

TABLE OF CONTENTS

**If you keep on doing
the same old thing,
you will keep on getting
the same old result.**

INTRODUCTION

Recently I worked with an unemployed person who had mailed out over 500 resumes with only one response. I told him that it was time to consider a new approach. If you have experienced some difficulties in getting hired into the job that you want, then it may be that you need a new approach as well. GET HIRED can provide you with an approach to help you be more successful.

In this book I will share with you many proven tips that I have learned over more than two decades in working with both students and unemployed adults who were searching for jobs. I will also share the results of my research with employers as I sought to better understand the most important factors employers look for when they hire new employees.

What are employers looking for when they hire?

The first chapter in this book will review your understanding of what job is best for you. In the first book in this series, CHOOSING YOUR CAREER, you were able to identify the career that is best for you (for high school students, you might have completed the book AFTER HIGH SCHOOL instead). Knowing what career you are looking for is critical to your future success. It is very difficult to write a cover letter or a resume if you don't have a clear picture of the career/job that is best for you. If you have any confusion over which career/job is right for you, I strongly recommend that you complete CHOOSING YOUR CAREER (or AFTER HIGH SCHOOL for high school students) before you begin to work in this book.

The second chapter can help you to better understand

what employers are looking for when they hire new employees. For example, a successful advertisement addresses the needs of potential customers. As you watch advertisements on television or view them in magazines, consider the thousands of dollars that have been spent in preparing these advertisements. A critical aspect of designing any advertisement focuses on the needs of the customer. Similarly in looking for a job, it is important for you to understand what employers are looking for. When your cover letter, resume and job interview answers meet the needs of the employer, you will experience greater success.

Chapters 3 to 9 will help you to identify your qualifications, skills, personal traits and accomplishments. As you complete these activities, it is important to take your time and complete each activity carefully. Eventually, the results from these activities will be used to help you write cover letters and resumes that can make a positive difference in your job search. In addition, the results from these activities will be used to help you better understand how to answer questions in job interviews.

Getting hired into the perfect career is primarily about selling yourself to an employer. Chapter 10 will give you some tips on marketing yourself. By the time you reach this chapter you will have a much better idea of what employers are looking for when they hire, and you will have a much better idea of how your skills and personal traits best satisfy the needs of employers. This chapter will help you to better understand how to look for a job in a manner that will help you to be more successful.

Chapter 11 will give you tips on writing effective cover letters.

Chapter 12 will give you tips on what to do and what not to do in writing a resume. It will also show you what you should include in your resume to make it stronger.

Chapter 13 can help you be more effective in a job interview. You will be given tips to help you prepare for a job interview as well as tips on handling the stress of a job interview. You will be given sample job interview questions and provided with appropriate responses for some of these questions.

An overall theme of this book is that there are basic steps to being successful in getting hired for the job that you desire, and that you are the person responsible for taking those steps in order to be successful.

Recently I was working with a woman who had been in the same job as a health care aide for more than 28 years. For most of these 28 years, she hated her job. She struggled to get out of bed in the morning to go to work. She experienced health problems as a result of the stress she felt working in a job she disliked. When I asked this woman why she chose her career, she replied that she didn't choose it, someone else chose it for her. After completing high school, she didn't know what she wanted to do with her future so when a friend told her she would be good working with sick people and there was a local agency hiring for jobs in this field, she listened. And that's exactly what she did for 28 years until she couldn't do it anymore. Unfortunately, by failing to take responsibility for her life and letting someone else decide what job would be best for her, this woman experienced 28 years of unhappiness in a career that wasn't suited to her.

Your future is your decision. Getting hired into the job

Taking your first step in the right direction is more important than taking many steps going the wrong way.

**The best way
to kill
an opportunity
is to avoid
taking it.**

of your dreams is your responsibility. I often tell unemployed people that finding the right job is a job in itself. There are no easy paths to getting hired into your perfect job. It will require some hard work and persistence on your part to be successful. Having said this, it is important to remain positive and expect the best.

GET HIRED can help you to be more successful. The content of this book is based on my work with thousands of people, many who achieved the career of their dreams by following the practical steps presented in this book. While the content of this book cannot guarantee success in getting hired, by following the tips and through the help of a career coach, counselor, or career advisor, you can increase your chances of being more successful.

TIPS ON ACHIEVING YOUR DREAMS

1. Write your dreams down.
Read them first thing in the morning and before you go to bed at night.

2. Visualize yourself as being successful in achieving your dreams.
Create a clear picture in your mind at all times of your success.

3. List all the ways you (and your family) will benefit when you
are successful in achieving your dreams.

4. Spend time with positive people who encourage and support you
in achieving your dreams.

5. Remember that success is not a spectator sport.
Action and achievement go hand in hand.

6. Your dreams will be best achieved when you break them down
into small, sequential steps that have appropriate and definite timelines.

7. When you encounter an obstacle,
look for a new way to achieve your end result.

8. Three key words to help you achieve your dreams are:
persistence, patience and purpose.

9. Learn from your failures.
Within each failure are clues to help you
to be more successful in achieving your dreams.

10. Reward yourself,
and celebrate each victory along the way.

What you focus on determines who you will be.

YOUR PERFECT CAREER

Do you have a clear picture of your perfect career? In one sentence, could you write an exact description of your dream career? Do you carry a statement of what you want to achieve in your wallet or purse? Do you have a picture of someone else being successful in this career? Is there someone you know who is successful in this career who is helping you to follow in his/her steps? These are all questions that are part of the first step in achieving the career that you want. You need to have a clear picture of the career you are seeking. Without this clear picture, it will be difficult to be successful in achieving the career of your dreams, and it will be easy to get hired into something that you really don't want to do.

For readers who don't have a clear picture of the career of your dreams, it is recommended that you complete CHOOSING YOUR CAREER, or for high school students - AFTER HIGH SCHOOL, before going any further in this book (additional information on these books is provided at the back of this book).

In the box below, state your perfect career (or write a sentence that best describes the kinds of things you would likely do in the career that would be best for you).

"If you can dream it, you can achieve it."
Walt Disney

MY PERFECT CAREER

On page 14, I would like you to paste or tape some sample job ads for the career that you identified at the bottom of page 11. This is a very important activity to complete as you will be referring back to these ads throughout this book. I strongly recommend that you also keep a "Career File" of any other ads you find related to your dream career and continually update this file by adding more ads to it. A file folder could be used as your career file.

To help you find your job advertisements, consider the tips provided on page 13.

TIPS ON FINDING YOUR PERFECT CAREER

1. Research websites of companies that you think might hire people for the job that you are seeking.

2. Contact Human Resources Departments.

3. Talk to people who already work in the job you are seeking.

4. Have someone who works in a company you are interested in check their company staff room bulletin boards.

5. Research career related websites such as:
www.monster.com
www.workopolis.com
(use internet searches to locate additional sites)

6. Check newspaper classified sections.

7. Use the telephone book to locate companies you might be interested in. Contact the companies to inquire where they advertise for new employees.

8. Read newspaper business sections for companies in the news who may be expanding their operations.

9. Use community career help services, employment agencies, and school guidance or placement services.

10. Locate trade publications and business directories. (often found in library reference departments)

11. Contact temporary job agencies.

12. Talk to friends, relatives, neighbors, teachers, coaches, etc.

13. Attend "Job Fairs".

14. If you are still in school, inquire whether you can pursue a co-op placement in your chosen field.

SAMPLE JOB ADVERTISEMENTS

Place additional ads in a file folder as you complete this book.

SUCCESS QUOTES

"Try not to become a man of success but rather try to become a man of value."
Albert Schweitzer

"Love the moment. Life is a succession of moments and to live each, is to succeed."
Corita Kent

"Success is not the key to happiness. Happiness is the key to success.
If you love what you are doing, you will be successful."
Albert Schweitzer

"The greatest reward for work well done is the opportunity to do more."
Jonas Salk

"Obstacles are those frightful things you see when you take your eyes off your goals."
Henry Ford

"The dictionary is the only place that success comes before work.
Hard work is the price we must pay for success."
Vince Lombardi

"Action is the foundational key to all success."
Pablo Picasso

"What would you attempt to do if you knew you would not fail?"
Robert Schuller

"People seldom see the slow and painful steps by which the most
insignificant success is achieved."
Anne Sullivan

"You don't have to stay up nights to be successful; you have to stay awake days."
Anonymous

"There are no secrets to success. It is the result of preparation, hard work,
and learning from failure."
Colin Powell

Understanding what the other side wants is one of the most important factors in getting what you want.

WHAT ARE EMPLOYERS LOOKING FOR?

Donald Trump has stated that one of the keys to any successful negotiation is understanding what the other side is looking for. Similarly, one of the keys to successfully getting hired into the career of your dreams is understanding what employers are looking for. Some people feel that a diploma or degree is a magic ticket into a great job. Unfortunately, this is rarely true.

During the past few years I have conducted ongoing research with companies continually asking the question, "What are you looking for when you hire new employees?" The answers to this question can be of great benefit to you as you seek employment. When you understand what employers are looking for, and when you present yourself (through your networking, cover letter, resume and interview answers) as the best person to meet these needs, you will find your greatest success.

Too many people in seeking jobs are constantly asking, "How can this company best help me?" The question you should be asking yourself is, "How can I best help this company?" When the answer to this question becomes the foundation of your search for your dream job, you will encounter greater success.

In asking companies what they are looking for when they hire new employees, the following six factors were those most frequently mentioned (and they are also in priority order with #1 being the factor that most employers stated was most important to them). In reading this list, it may be useful to realize that some jobs and some

The most important question to be asking yourself is, "How can I best help this company?"

companies may rank these factors in a slightly different order and may even add additional factors. As will be explained later in this book, your research into a company and your careful reading of a job ad can provide clues as to what a company is looking for in selecting new employees. For now, this list provides an excellent start for you to begin to think about in deciding how you can best market yourself in terms of meeting the needs of potential employers.

1. **TRAINING/QUALIFICATIONS**
2. **POSITIVE ATTITUDE**
3. **EXPERIENCE**
4. **PEOPLE SKILLS**
5. **WORK ETHIC**
6. **ADAPTABLE**

When you consider each of these six factors every time you apply for a job (integrating these into your cover letter, resume, networking, and interviews), you can be more successful. In the remainder of this book, I will show you how to do this. By the end of this book you can have a cover letter, a resume and even answers to the major questions you will be asked in an interview that best match your strengths and what companies are looking for.

Applying for a job is a form of marketing. You are marketing yourself. Similar to any other form of marketing, you will be more successful if you understand the needs of your customers. In this case, your customer is your future employer. Take time to research their needs. Clues regarding their needs are found in job ads, company websites, newspaper/magazine articles regarding trends in your industry, and most of all by talking to people who are already in the career you are attempting to get hired into.

GOAL QUOTES

"A goal properly set is halfway reached."
Abraham Lincoln

"For me, goals are my road to the life I want.
They have helped me to accomplish things I once thought were impossible."
Catherine Pulsifer

"Whoever wants to reach a distant goal must take small steps."
Helmut Schmidt

"All successful people have a goal. No one can get anywhere
unless he knows where he wants to go and what he wants to be or do."
Norman Vincent Peale

"The tragedy of life doesn't lie in not reaching your goal.
The tragedy lies in having no goals to reach."
Benjamin Mays

"The most important thing about goals is having one."
Geoffry. F. Abert

"In achieving your goals, you may run into roadblocks.
Don't let that stop you. Go around, over, or under.
If you are committed to your goal you will find a way."
Catherine Pulsifer

"You have to know what you want before you can get it."
Gertrude Stein

"Look to the future, because that is where you will spend the rest of your life."
G. Burns

"The choices we make are ultimately our own responsibility."
Eleanor Roosevelt

For many employers, your degree, diploma or certificate is a basic necessity to even be considered for a job.

WHAT ARE YOUR QUALIFICATIONS?

In my research with employers, 93.8% of them stated that the number one consideration in hiring new employees related to their qualifications and/or training credentials. What this really means is employers are looking for something concrete such as a diploma, certificate, license, or degree that proves that you have achieved a minimum standard required for the job they are advertising. In most cases, if you don't have this minimum standard you are wasting your time applying for the job. In fact, in my research with employers, one of the major concerns they have with people applying for jobs relates to those who apply for jobs even when they are not qualified. As you begin to market yourself to employers you want them to immediately recognize that you have the qualifications they are looking for.

As you begin to think about your qualifications, it is important to realize that your qualifications are different than your skills. For example, typing 60 words a minute is a skill while graduating from a secretarial program states your qualifications. Knowing how to motivate children is a skill while completing a teacher education program proves your qualifications. Knowing how to wire a house is a skill while having completed an apprenticeship program as an electrician provides your qualifications.   In Chapter 4, you will explore your skills. In this chapter you are going to identify your qualifications.

In general, your qualifications can be shown by providing a certificate, diploma, license, or degree (or some other official piece of paper) that certifies that you have

**You want the employer
to immediately recognize
that you have the qualifications they
are looking for.**

completed a required program in an accredited school or training facility. A basic qualification for most people will be a high school diploma. Beyond this, what qualifications have you successfully completed?

As you consider job advertisements, look closely for the educational level or training qualifications required for the jobs you are interested in. When you find a job that you might be interested in but you lack the qualifications, ask yourself whether you are prepared to gain these qualifications? If your answer is "no", then it might be in your best interest to begin to look for other jobs that you are qualified for.

Once you have identified your qualifications, it is also important to identify the name of the school or training facility where you completed these qualifications, and also the date you graduated or completed the training. This information will be added to your resume later.

Re-read the job advertisements from your career file (see page 14). As you read the ads again, look carefully for the educational or training requirements identified for these jobs. In CHART A below, list the educational level or training qualifications required for the careers(s) you are most interested in, and then underline any of these qualifications that you actually have.

The most successful advertisements immediately capture a customer's interests.

CHART A - QUALIFICATIONS REQUIRED

GOAL SETTING TIPS

1. The most important thing about setting your goals is having one.

2. Write your goals and look at them often.

3. Take action. A goal without action is still just a dream.

4. Use a journal to keep track of your results as you work towards achieving your goals.

5. List all the ways you will benefit from achieving your goals.

6. Write a step-by-step plan for reaching your goals.

7. Set specific deadlines for achieving your goals and also for completing each step along the way.

8. Talk to someone you respect and trust about your goals and your plans to achieve them.

9. Prioritize your goals so that you know which one is most important.

10. Spend most of your time working on your most important goal.

You will be more successful
in selling yourself
when employers understand
the benefits they will gain
by hiring you.

WHAT ARE YOUR SKILLS?

Your education, training, and previous work experiences helped you to gain specific skills. A dictionary might define "skill" as:

  - expertise, practiced ability, something you do well

A thesaurus might define "skill" as:

  - ability, adroitness, aptitude, competence, handiness, technique

Your skills are the things that you can do well. In applying for a job it is important to first of all identify the skills the employer is looking for. Next, you need to identify the skills that you have that best match what the employer is looking for. One of the biggest mistakes many job hunters make in their resumes is to list everything they have done or can possibly do. As you will learn throughout this book, you will be more successful in getting hired into the job of your dreams when you focus your efforts on meeting the needs of your future employer.

In this chapter you are going to focus on your skills in two areas:

1) SPECIFIC JOB RELATED

2) PERSONAL

You will be more successful in getting hired into the job of your dreams when you focus your efforts on meeting the needs of your future employer.

Before you begin to write a resume, a cover letter, or even apply for a job, create a profile of what employers are looking for in the career you are seeking.

1) The following are examples of specific job related skills employers might be looking for in a variety of jobs:

- proficient in using Microsoft Office Professional
- ability to install and maintain electrical equipment
- exceptional Excel skills
- knowledge of fabrication techniques
- experience in all phases of installation procedures
- good record keeping strategies
- strong database management skills
- driving experience
- can assemble mechanical components
- sound knowledge of related systems
- strong computer skills

2) The following are examples of personal skills employers are looking for in a variety of jobs:

- able to work in a fast-paced environment.
- able to work with minimal supervision
- strong organizational, problem solving
and communication skills
- experience working with the public
- effectively manages time and priorities
- ability to follow policies and procedures
- enthusiasm
- above average customer service skills
- team player

Instead of asking you to list all the skills you have learned, I would like you to first of all think about what employers are looking for in the career you would like to have. To do this, return to your job advertisements from your career file (or the ones you posted on page 14). Read each advertisement carefully once again.

From the ads, identify the skills that are most frequently mentioned. After you have done this, list the most frequently mentioned specific job related skills on CHART B below and then the most frequently mentioned personal skills required for the job on CHART C below (if you need a bigger space to write in for either, or both charts, use a separate sheet of paper and then glue it or tape it on this page).

Throughout this book, you will learn that your resume, cover letter, and job interview will all be stronger when you give supporting evidence (proof) of anything you state about yourself. On page 29 you will begin to explore how you can best prove you have the skills that you think best describe you.

"Some of us will do our jobs well and some will not, but we will be judged by only one thing: the result."
Vince Lombardi

CHART B - SPECIFIC JOB RELATED SKILLS

CHART C - PERSONAL SKILLS

IDENTIFYING
YOUR BEST SKILLS

There are two factors to consider in identifying your best skills. First of all, what are the skills the employer is seeking? Second, which of the skills the employer is seeking are the ones you are most proficient in? It is also important to be able to give specific examples from previous jobs (school and/or training) that support your claims.

On page 27 you identified the job specific skills and personal skills that were most frequently mentioned in job ads for the career you are most interested in. Your next task to help you get hired into your perfect career is to choose the skills that best describe you, and then think of an example that illustrates you successfully using the skill mentioned.

To do this, select the 2 skills from CHART B and the 2 skills from CHART C on page 27 that best describe you. Then list these 4 skills in the left hand column on CHART D on page 29 (if you need more space, complete this activity on a separate piece of paper and then glue this into your book).

After you have done this, in the right hand column of CHART D write examples of things you have done (in a former job or in your training/education for the job) that prove you actually have each of these skills. For example, if you state you are proficient in using Microsoft Office Professional then talk about a specific project/assignment you completed that proves this is a strong skill for you. If you state that you work well with little supervision, once again write a specific example of a project/assignment that you completed where there was little or no supervision.

"Actions speak louder than words"
Proverbs

CHART D - IDENTIFYING YOUR BEST SKILLS

SKILLS	PROOF THAT YOU HAVE THESE SKILLS

Later in this book, we will return back to the information you wrote on this page so you can see how this information can be applied to your resume, job interviews and your networking with others.

Positive people
believe
they will be successful.

DEVELOPING
A POSITIVE ATTITUDE

In my research with employers the number one personal trait that employers desire in an employee is positive attitude. Interestingly, the number one personal trait that employees value in co-workers is also a positive attitude. What is positive attitude? How can you determine your attitude? How can you improve this important part of yourself? This chapter will consider this important aspect of getting hired into the job that you desire.

There are three major characteristics of positive people. These are:

1) **They are 100% responsible for how they live.**
2) **They see obstacles as temporary.**
3) **They view themselves as being successful.**

On this and the following page you will have an opportunity to learn more about each of these three characteristics of positive people.

1. 100% RESPONSIBLE

One of the major themes in my book CHOOSING YOUR CAREER is that you can decide to live your life the way you want to live it or you can allow other people to tell you what to do, even if you are uncomfortable or unhappy with what they decide for you. How you live your life is your choice. Yes, there may be things that happen to you that you didn't want, but in the end how you react to these unfortunate experiences is your choice.

People with a positive attitude accept 100% responsibility for their lives. They don't blame others for their failures. They accept personal responsibility for both

> "The greatest
> discovery
> of all time
> is that a person
> can change
> his future
> by merely
> changing
> his attitude."
> Oprah Winfrey

successes and failures. When they try something and it doesn't work out the way they had hoped, instead of trying to find someone else to blame, they consider what they can learn from the experience and then begin again by adjusting their actions.

You have the power to create you own world. You can write your own script for living, but first you have to take responsibility for doing it instead of letting others decide how you should live or what you should do.

2. TEMPORARY OBSTACLES

Do positive people ever get discouraged? Absolutely. It is normal to feel frustration and even anger when things aren't going the way you had hoped. If you are currently looking for a job, you may be experiencing these types of feelings. Unemployment can be a difficult time in anyone's life. Unfortunately, it is generally easier to stay in a discouraged state then it is to overcome these feelings. And the longer a person remains discouraged, the greater the likelihood that this will become a mental habit that can sabotage any opportunities to become successful.

Positive people view obstacles as setbacks. In fact, many positive people, after the initial anger or frustration that comes from obstacles, immediately begin to look for some good that might come out of the problem. Perhaps, there's an opportunity - a silver lining in a dark cloud - that might come their way. Perhaps, for you, being unemployed may be an opportunity to find a job that will fill you with passion and purpose.

3. VISION OF BEING SUCCESSFUL

What we think about the most is who we become. Unfortunately, the experts in human psychology tell us that most people are basically negative thinkers. To become a positive thinker, you need to have a clear picture in your mind of being successful. It may help you to write out a few sentences describing your eventual success, or you might even find some pictures that best illustrate the kind of person you would like to be (including family and career possibilities). People with a positive attitude have a very clear picture of their goals, both daily and long term. Positive people see themselves as being successful. Whenever doubts creep into their mind, they replace the negative thoughts with crystal clear pictures of being successful.

This vision of being successful helps positive people to remain calm and optimistic when other people see a situation as being bleak.

On CHART E below, the left hand side provides 10 characteristics of positive people. Read the characteristics, and then on the right hand side of this chart list the characteristics as they best describe you with #1 being the characteristic that best describes you, #2 the next best, and so on.

> "If we are basically positive in attitude, expecting and envisioning pleasure, satisfaction and happiness, we will attract people, and create situations and events which conform to our positive expectations."
> Shakti Gawain

CHART E - MY POSITIVE TRAITS

EASY TO GET ALONG WITH	1. . . . .
DOESN'T BLAME OTHERS	2. . . . .
RARELY COMPLAINS	3. . . . .
TENDS TO BE HAPPY	4. . . . .
TREATS OTHERS FAIRLY	5. . . . .
TENDS TO BE OPTIMISTIC	6. . . . .
EXCELLENT PROBLEM SOLVER	7. . . . .
STRONG SELF-DISCIPLINE	8. . . . .
CAN BE RELIED ON	9. . . . .
ACHIEVES GOALS	10. . . . .

QUOTES RELATED TO POSITIVE ATTITUDE

"Optimism is the one quality more associated with success
and happiness than any other."
Brian Tracy

"Your own mind is a sacred enclosure into which nothing
harmful can enter except by your permission."
Ralph Waldo Emerson

"I have had dreams and I have had nightmares,
but I have conquered my nightmares because of my dreams."
Dr. Jonas Salk

"If I keep a green bough in my heart, the singing bird will come."
Chinese Proverb

"The optimist sees opportunity in every danger;
the pessimist sees danger in every opportunity."
Winston Churchill

"Happiness is an attitude. We either make ourselves miserable, or happy
and strong. The amount of work is the same."
Francesca Reigler

"There is a little difference in people, but that little difference
makes a big difference.
That little difference is attitude.
The big difference is whether it is positive or negative."
W. Clement Stone

"All our dreams can come true - if we have the courage to pursue them."
Walt Disney

"You must do the thing you think you cannot do."
Eleanor Roosevelt

"I am not discouraged,
because every wrong attempt discarded is another step forward."
Thomas Edison

NETWORKING TIPS

As you begin to look for your perfect job, you will constantly be talking to others (whether it's family, relatives, neighbors, friends, potential employers, etc.). This is known as "networking". As you network with others (even if you don't think they have any connection with someone who may hire you), always present yourself as someone who is optimistic and also someone who is qualified for the job that you are seeking.

Whenever you create a positive impression with someone, you will be quickly remembered if this person knows another person who might be able to help you in your job search. If you create a negative impression by complaining about how hard it is to find a job or just by being generally pessimistic, this person might listen to your concerns, but then make a mental note not to ever recommend you to someone who might be able to help you.

You never know who might provide a personal link to a potential employer, so strive to impress everyone that you talk to.

In addition, whenever someone takes the time to help you in your job search it would be beneficial for you to send them a thank-you card. People like to receive cards that thank them for making an extra effort to help someone else. Often, such a card may be posted in the person's office and becomes a reminder of your desire to find the job of your dreams.

By sending a thank-you card, you are helping to enhance your image as a positive person who is willing to give thanks and acknowledge the efforts of others.

You can purchase blank thank-you cards at most drug stores or stationary stores. Don't choose a card that is too flashy or uses humor that could be interpreted the wrong way. Simply find a card that says thank you. If possible, use a quality printer to print your name, address, telephone number and email address inside the card.

And don't forget as you thank the person to remind them once again of the actual job you are seeking.

A valued employee
gets along well
with co-workers.

IMPROVE YOUR PEOPLE SKILLS

It is difficult to find any job today that does not require an employee to have effective people skills. In my research with employees the number one cause of stress identified in the workplace stems from conflict between co-workers (see the chart below). Employees with strong people skills are valued by employers, co-workers and customers/clients.

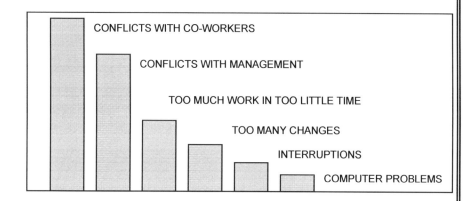

> "Alone we can do so little, together we can do so much."
> Helen Keller

An important aspect of selecting a successful job candidate for most employers relates to finding someone who will fit into the company atmosphere. Tips are provided in this chapter to help you this chapter can also help you to better understand various aspects of people skills.

Too many people in applying for jobs vaguely mention something about people skills without really considering what this means. As recommended in previous chapters, a job application becomes much stronger when an applicant can provide specific examples to support whatever claims he/she is making. In the area of people skills, what are the specific things you should be paying attention to to make this aspect of your job search stronger?

For example, listening has often been identified as one of the most important communication skills that contributes to positive relationships with others. Good listening skills help people to understand others and identify their needs. This not only helps reduce workplace conflict, but also improves productivity by eliminating problems associated with mistakes being made because of poor communications. The tips provided in this chapter related to handling workplace conflict can also help you to better understand some specific listening techniques.

"People with goals succeed because they know where they are going."
Earl Nightingale

"Researchers have identified the core factors in a happy life. The primary components focus on the closeness of your relationships with family and other people."
David Niven
(The 100 Simple Secrets of Happy People")

TIPS ON FITTING IN

1. Find something good to say
about others if you have to say anything at all.

2. Do what you say you are going to do.
Honesty brings respect.

3. Show concern for the feelings of others.

4. Listen to others as they share their interests and ideas.

5. Be a positive person.
Leave your aches, pains and problems at home.

6. Be an optimistic person.
Look for the best in any situation instead of the worst.

7. Keep an open mind.
Learn to accept the differences in other people.

8. When you are presenting your point of view,
remain calm and deal with the facts.

9. Be quick to forgive.
If you have to confront a co-worker (or boss)
concerning a problem, do it in private
and at the convenience of the other person.

10. Take pride in your work
without feeling the need to boast about it.

TIPS ON DEALING WITH WORKPLACE CONFLICT

1. Be proactive. Ignoring potential conflicts
can allow them to escalate.

2. Be slow to anger - especially over little things.
Listen before you speak. If necessary, go for a walk
or spend some time alone to relax before you deal with the conflict.

3. If you find that you are wrong, admit it. On the other hand, if you
are not wrong, be assertive in voicing your needs and rights.
Do not neglect your own needs in order to make other people happy.

4. Look at yourself first before you blame others.
Is there something you can do to resolve the concern
before it actually becomes a full blown problem?

5. Look for common ground as quickly as possible.

6. Attempt to understand the other person's point of view
rather than attempting to convince him/her of yours.
The most effective listening skill to use in understanding
another person is to paraphrase what he/she is telling you.

7. Where emotions are involved, let other people express
their feelings before you attempt to resolve the problem.

8. Attempt to handle the conflict in private instead of in front
of your co-workers. Avoid having anyone involved in the
conflict being embarrassed in front of others.

9. Avoid exaggerations, either in your mind or in what you say.
Attempt to keep your thoughts and words based on fact.

10. Look for solutions where both sides benefit.

IDENTIFYING
YOUR BEST PEOPLE SKILLS

On pages 39 + 40 are tips that reflect strong people skills. Re-read each of these pages and complete the charts below.

On CHART F list the two statements from page 39 that best describe how you would successfully fit into a new company environment. You can rephrase the statements in your own words.

CHART F - FITTING INTO A NEW COMPANY

1.

2.

On CHART G list the two statements from page 40 that best describe how you would successfully handle a conflict in the workplace. You can rephrase the statements in your own words.

CHART G - DEALING WITH CONFLICTS

1.

2.

**You will find
your greatest success
when you spend most
of your time doing
the things you do best.**

IDENTIFYING YOUR WORK ETHIC

It is a given that employers would like to hire someone who is a hard worker, and as result someone who improves the company's profits. Hard work is often associated with the term "work ethic", but there are other factors that come under the umbrella of this term as well. For example, reliability, responsibility, punctuality, and self-starter are some of the factors that are also associated with work ethic.

Below are some of the common work ethic traits that employers seek. Re-read the job advertisements you placed in your career file or on page 14 and put a check mark beside each trait below that is listed in one of your job advertisements. There is also additional space for you to list any other work ethic traits from your advertisements that are not listed below.

"Opportunity is missed by most because it is dressed in overalls and looks like work."
Thomas Edison

- ABILITY TO PRIORITIZE
- ABILITY TO WORK IN A FAST-PACED ENVIRONMENT
- ABLE TO MULTI-TASK
- ACHIEVES GOALS
- ATTENTION TO DETAIL
- COMPLETES PROJECTS
- ENTHUSIASTIC
- FOLLOWS DIRECTIONS
- PROBLEM SOLVING SKILLS
- PUNCTUAL

- QUICK LEARNER
- RELIABLE
- RESPONSIBLE
- SELF-DIRECTED
- SELF-STARTER
- TIME MANAGEMENT SKILLS
- WELL ORGANIZED
-
-
-

On CHART H below, list the three work ethic traits from the list on page 43 that best describe you.

```
┌─────────────────────────────────────────────┐
│                                             │
│        CHART H - WORK ETHIC TRAITS          │
│                                             │
│                                             │
│                                             │
│                                             │
│                                             │
│                                             │
└─────────────────────────────────────────────┘
```

On page 45 are some quotes related to work ethic.

On page 46 are some tips to help you better manage your time and on 47 some tips related to being more organized, both common work ethic characteristics desired by employers.

From page 45, select a quote that best describes you and write it in the box below.

```
┌─────────────────────────────────────────────┐
│                                             │
│           A WORK ETHIC QUOTE                │
│         THAT BEST DESCRIBES ME              │
│                                             │
│                                             │
│                                             │
│                                             │
│                                             │
│                                             │
└─────────────────────────────────────────────┘
```

"Work is either fun or drudgery. It all depends on your attitude."
Colleen C. Barrett

WORK ETHIC QUOTES

"I have missed more than 9,000 shots in my career.
I have lost almost 300 games. On 26 occasions I have been entrusted
to take the game winning shot ... and I missed.
I have failed over and over and over again in my life.
And that's precisely why I succeed."
Michael Jordan

"Nothing will ever be attempted if all possible objections
must first be overcome."
Samuel Johnson

"Doing the best at this moment
puts you in the best place for the next moment."
Oprah Winfrey

"Opportunity is missed by most because
it is dressed in overalls and looks like work."
Thomas Edison

"If people knew how hard I have to work to gain my mastery,
it wouldn't seem wonderful at all."
Michelangelo

"I'm a great believer in luck,
and I find the harder I work, the more I have of it."
Thomas Jefferson

"The only place where success comes before work is in the dictionary."
Vidal Sassoon

"I long to accomplish great and noble tasks, but it is my chief duty
to accomplish humble tasks as though they were great and noble."
Helen Keller

"The secret of joy in work is contained in one word - excellence."
Pearl S. Buck

"Pleasure in the job puts perfection in the work."
Aristotle

TIME MANAGEMENT TIPS

1. It takes less time to fix a problem before it happens.

2. Faster is not always better.

3. Working smarter is more important than working longer.

4. Judging others usually takes up more of your time than accepting them.

5. Do it right the first time.

6. A few minutes at the end of each day to organize yourself
for tomorrow will generally take less time
than if you leave this for tomorrow.

7. You will generally be more productive
if you keep your schedule somewhere else than in your head.

8. Before you begin any task,
ensure that you understand what you are to do.

9. Interruptions are only interruptions
when you permit them to be that.

10. Prioritize all the tasks that you need to do,
and then start with the highest priority first.

11. Learn to say "NO".

12. There are times when doing something well
is better than doing something perfectly.

13. Make a "TO DO" list every day.

14. By reducing the amount of time you procrastinate,
you will have more time to get things done.

15. Analyze how you use your time,
and eliminate the timewasters.

TIPS FOR BEING BETTER ORGANIZED

1. Be prepared ahead of time. For example, before going to bed at night, plan what you are going to wear tomorrow and have all required materials for the day ready to go.

2. Use color-coded file folders to organize your tasks and assignments. For example, you might use a different color file for each day of the week.

3. Use a date/day book to keep track of deadlines for all projects and assignments. Keep this book with you all the time and always write down anything that you need to remember to do. Check the book each day to ensure that you are aware of all deadlines that are approaching.

4. Use a daily "TO DO" list. Prioritize what you have to do and start with your most difficult tasks. Enter approximate times for completing each task. Whenever you complete a task on your "TO DO" list, cross out the item to show it is completed.

5. Have a specific place where you keep things. For example, always put your keys in the same place and you will never waste time looking for them again.

6. Enter your most frequently used telephone numbers into your telephone memory so they are always quickly available.

7. Use a drawer organizer to keep track of things such as scissors, paper clips, glue, pens, pencils, etc.

8. Back up your computer files on a regular basis.

9. Every time you buy something new, get rid of something old.

10. Leave so you will arrive early. In the same way, schedule more time to complete tasks than you think they will take.

Progress
is a product of change.

IMPORTANCE OF BEING ADAPTABLE

We are living at a time when technological changes are occurring so quickly that it is often difficult to keep up with the pace. For anyone entering the workplace, the ability to deal effectively with change is an important attribute for success. In some companies, job roles change frequently. In addition, technological changes can affect the way things are done. A person who becomes bewildered or overly stressed by such changes can lose his/her value to a company. As employers hire new workers, they value people with a proven record of welcoming change.

Below, list 3 changes you have experienced either in a present or former job (students could use a part-time job or even changes that occurred at school). These changes might includes things like having to adapt to new computer software, or new rules/policies, or having to do something in a different manner after having done it another way for a long period of time.

1.

2.

3.

CHAPTER

8

"It is not the strongest who survive, nor the most intelligent, but the one who is most responsive to change."
Charles Darwin

Read the TIPS FOR DEALING WITH CHANGE that are provided on page 51. After reading these tips, select the 2 tips that you think best describe the way you successfully dealt with any or all of the 3 changes you listed on page 49.

Write these 2 tips in your own words on CHART I below.

"Growth itself
contains
the germ
of happiness."
Pearl S. Buck

> **CHART I - DEALING WITH CHANGE**
>
> 1.
>
> 2.

Read the "Change Quotes" that are provided on page 52. After reading these tips, select a quote that you think would be a positive way for you to handle change. Write this quote in the box below.

> **A QUOTE THAT DESCRIBES A POSITIVE WAY TO DEAL WITH CHANGE**

Finally, on page 53 is a letter for you to write to yourself about dealing with changes that you will be facing in your life. Complete the letter.

TIPS FOR DEALING WITH CHANGE

1. Look for the opportunities and benefits
that the change can bring to you.

2. Don't waste energy on resisting change
if it's going to happen anyway.

3. Decide how to react to change rather than letting others
tell you how they think you should react.

4. Take responsibility for changing yourself,
not others.

5. Keep things in perspective.
We often allow things to become
much worse in our mind than they actually are.

6. Focus on what you can control, not what you cannot.

7. Learn how to deal with the stress of change
by employing techniques such as exercise or meditation.

8. Explore the different choices you have related to the change.

9. Get all the information related to the change
and attempt to understand it before you react.

10. Identify the emotions you are feeling,
and deal with them before you attempt
to work through the change.

CHANGE QUOTES

"If you don't like something, change it;
if you can't change it, change the way you think about it."
Mary Engelbreit

"When we are no longer able to change a situation,
we are challenged to change ourselves."
Victor Frankl

"Without accepting the fact that everything changes,
we cannot find perfect composure."
Shunryu Suzuki

"God grant me the serenity to accept the people I cannot change,
the courage to change the one I can, and the wisdom to know it's me."
Anonymous

"The world hates change,
yet it is the only thing that has brought progress."
Charles Kettering

"Change is the law of life. And those who look only to the past
or present are certain to miss the future."
J. F. Kennedy

""The truth is that our finest moments are more likely to occur when
we are feeling deeply uncomfortable, unhappy, or unfilled. For it is only
in such moments, propelled by our discomfort, that we are likely
to step out of our rut and start seeking a different way or truer answers."
M. Scott Peck

"Our universe is transformation; our life is what our thoughts make of it."
Marcus Aurellius

"Life is progress, and not a station."
Ralph Waldo Emerson

A LETTER TO MYSELF ABOUT CHANGE

Dear Me,

    Over the next year or two some changes that I know I will be facing are

    Some of the ways that I can deal with these changes in a positive manner are

Some people who can help me to better deal with these changes are

Take pride
in your accomplishments.

IDENTIFYING YOUR ACCOMPLISHMENTS

The previous chapters have described your qualifications, your skills, your attitude, and your work ethic. What you do with these personal attributes become your accomplishments. Your accomplishments are actual proof that you are able to employ your qualifications, your skills, your attitude and work ethic to do something meaningful.

In your cover letter, resume and job interview, employers are looking for specific things you have accomplished in previous jobs (for students, part-time jobs or school/community related accomplishments can be used). These accomplishments support the other things you have said about yourself.

Examples of your accomplishments might be projects or tasks you completed (whether as an individual or part of a team) that you felt really good about. Accomplishments may also include new ideas or proposals that you made that resulted in concrete products or improvements of some form. Accomplishments may also include successfully solving problems, whether product or people related. In addition, accomplishments could include anything you did that improved the company profile in a positive way or increased company profits.

In some situations, your accomplishments may have resulted in you receiving an award or some other form of recognition (prize, bonus, media coverage, letter, verbal congratulations, etc.). Such accomplishments are the best ones to use when you are trying to make a positive impact on a future employer.

"Most of the important things in the world have been accomplished by people who have kept trying when there seemed to be no hope at all."
Dale Carnegie

On CHART J below, identify three accomplishments that you feel best represent things that you are proudest of at work (could also include community and/or volunteer work).

CHART J
THREE PROUD ACCOMPLISHMENTS FOR ME

1.

2.

3.

ACCOMPLISHMENT QUOTES

"In the confrontation between the stream and the rock,
the stream always wins, not by strength but through perseverance."
H. J. Brown

"It is by what we ourselves have done,
and not by what others have done for us,
that we shall be remembered in after ages."
Francis Wayland

"It is not so important who starts the game but who finishes it."
John Wooden

"To be yourself in a world that is constantly trying to make you
something else is the greatest accomplishment."
Ralph Waldo Emerson

"Discipline is the bridge between goals and accomplishment."
Jim Rohn

"Nothing stops the man who desires to achieve.
Every obstacle is simply a course to develop his achievement muscle."
Eric Butterworth

"Not everyone desires to be a bank president or a nuclear scientist,
but everyone wants to do something with one's life
that will give him a sense of pride and accomplishment."
Ronald Regan

"Every great work, every big accomplishment
has been brought into manifestation
through holding to the vision, and often just before the big achievement,
comes apparent failure and discouragement."
Florence Shinn

**The manner in which
you market yourself
says a lot about the kind
of employee you will be.**

TIPS FOR MARKETING YOURSELF

Throughout the first nine chapters of this book you have learned more about what employers are looking for when they hire. In addition, you have identified your strengths related to each of the major factors employers are looking for. In review, the six major factors employers are looking for when they hire are:

1. **TRAINING/QUALIFICATIONS**

2. **POSITIVE ATTITUDE**

3. **EXPERIENCE**

4. **PEOPLE SKILLS**

5. **WORK ETHIC**

6. **ADAPTABLE**

Success for most businesses ultimately depends on understanding the needs of their customers/clients and delivering a product or service that best fulfills those needs at a competitive price. Successful job searching is very similar. You need to identify what companies are looking for, and then present yourself in a way to convince employers that you can best meet these needs.

The information you have thought about, and the questions you have answered in previous chapters in this book, will now provide the basis for you to successfully market yourself to potential employers. A guiding rule of thumb should be to present your qualifications, skills, experience,

CHAPTER

10

> **"The aim of marketing is to know and understand the customer so well that the product or service sells itself."**
> Peter F. Drucker

accomplishments, attitude and work ethic as it best matches what a specific company that you are applying to is looking for. Remember that job advertisements, company websites, newspaper/magazine articles, and contact with people who work for or with the company will give you clues as to what the company is looking for.

The following page provides some tips on marketing yourself. As you complete the remaining chapters of this book you will begin to better understand how you can best employ these tips in your cover letter, resume and in answering questions in a job interview.

One of the most effective ways to get the job you want is through personal contact with other people. In the box below, write the names of some key people who you feel could help you to gain employment into your perfect career. It is recommended that you spend some time with these people asking them to support and help you.

"Overused words do not work. Offer the compelling stories - the case studies, awards, business growth, achievements - that make those adjectives unnecessary."
Harry Beckwith

SOME KEY PEOPLE WHO COULD HELP ME

TIPS FOR MARKETING YOURSELF

1. First impressions are important.
Always create a positive image of yourself.

2. Dress for success.

3. Take care of yourself through good eating,
sleeping and exercise habits.

4. Set a daily schedule that outlines
your goals each day in looking for a job.

5. Work hard at understanding exactly
what a company is looking for
and then match your results throughout this book
to meet these needs.

6. Learn as much as you can about the company you are applying to.
Ask yourself how you can contribute to this company's success.

7. Identify someone who either works for or knows someone
who works for the company you are interested in.
Talk to this person about the company's needs.

8. Form a buddy group with other people who are looking for a job.
Help each other with job searching, resumes, practice interviews, etc.

9. Be persistent, but also be willing to change your approach
if you are not getting the results you would like.

10. Learn to network.
Be positive with everyone you talk to about getting a job.

**Your cover letter
often creates the
first impression of you.**

WRITING EFFECTIVE COVER LETTERS

For many people who are searching for a job, the first contact with a potential employer is often in the form of a letter known as a cover letter. Generally, this letter is accompanied by a resume.

The cover letter creates a first impression. A well-designed cover letter can gain a prospective employer's attention and influence them to read further. A poorly written cover letter might prevent the employer from even looking at your resume or consider you for a job interview. Often, job searchers spend hours of time working on a resume while rushing through a cover letter. A well written cover letter that is neat and professional looking suggests that the writer is well prepared and professional. A strong cover letter can have a positive effect on how the resume is read.

Cover letters may be written in response to a job advertisement, or may be a written form of cold calling often called a "broadcast letter" in which case you are writing to inquire about job positions that have not even been advertised.

It is not the purpose of this book to provide endless examples of cover letters that you can copy. You can find examples of cover letters by typing "cover letter" into your search engine on the internet. Some websites that can provide help for you related to writing cover letters are listed on the right hand side of this page, although this list is by no means comprehensive.

CHAPTER
11

"Vision without action is a daydream."
Japanese Proverb

www.workopolis.com
www.monster.com
www.bestcoverletters.com
www.jobstar.org
www.vault.com
www.jobbankusa.com

**Attention
to the
smallest details
can sometimes
make
the biggest
difference.**

The main purpose of this brief chapter is to help you understand the content that is important to have in your cover letter. On page 66 is a general outline for a cover letter with suggestions you can use to make your cover letter more effective. This outline incorporates your strengths in relationship to the needs of employers. The best way to market yourself is always to be asking "How can I help this company?" If you answer this question in your cover letter, resume, and in the interview, you will be more successful in obtaining the job of your dreams.

On page 65 are some tips to help you write a great cover letter. After writing your cover letter, re-read each of these tips and ensure that you have followed each suggestion.

You might also find it beneficial to read the tips for writing a resume which are provided on page 73. Some of these tips also apply to writing your cover letter. Both your cover letter and resume become stronger when they look and read like they belong together.

In addition, it is important that you realize there can be different types of letters you might send to an employer. Some of the types are:

- broadcast
- cover or response letter
- networking letter
- thank you letter

These types of letters are explained in more detail on page 67.

TIPS ON WRITING AN EFFECTIVE COVER LETTER

1. Target your letter to the employer's needs.
Before you start your letter, make a list of what the employer
wants (this book has given you many ideas as to what employers
are looking for) and then write a sentence or two
to explain how you can meet each of these needs.

2. Keep your cover letter to one page.

3. Proofread spelling and grammar.

4. Ensure that you have told the employer
exactly what job/career you are applying for.

5. Address the letter (where possible) to a real person
instead of using "To Whom It Concerns".

6. Use 1" margins around the page.
Use quality 8 1/2 X 11" white paper to print on.
Use the best printer you have access to.
Use a standard font (such as Times New Roman or Arial)
instead of using some fancy font that may be hard to read.
In addition, keep your font size for the text around 12
while your name, address, etc. may be 14. Don't use
more than two fonts throughout the letter. Use black ink.

7. Include specific examples as much as possible
to illustrate anything you say.

8. Explain what you can offer the company,
not what the company can do for you.

9. Avoid faxing or emailing the letter unless you are
specifically instructed to do it this way.

10. State in your letter that your resume is also included.

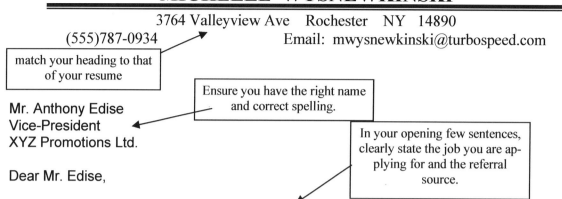

MICHELLE WYSNEWKINSKI

3764 Valleyview Ave   Rochester   NY   14890

(555)787-0934   Email: mwysnewkinski@turbospeed.com

match your heading to that
of your resume

Mr. Anthony Edise
Vice-President
XYZ Promotions Ltd.

Ensure you have the right name
and correct spelling.

Dear Mr. Edise,

In your opening few sentences, clearly state the job you are applying for and the referral source.

Recently, I viewed your advertisement for the position of Public Relations Manager in the Vancouver Sun. After speaking to John Heatherington, who currently works in HR at XYZ Promotions Ltd., I have decided that I would like to apply for the Public Relations Manager position.

For the past three years I have worked as the Assistant Public Relations Manager at Kelly Marketing Group. In this position I thrived on the

Two paragraphs in your main body is sufficient. Attempt to match your skills to those requested in the job advertisement. Where possible, provide specific examples of accomplishments to illustrate what you are saying (CHART J on page 56) Focus on how you can help the company.

fast pace of the work environment. My time management, organizational and problem solving skills have been of tremendous assistance to me in helping Kelly Marketing Group achieve their target goals. As an example, our New Customer Attraction Team, of which I was the chairperson, increased our customer base by 36.3% over two years which exceeded our goals. I have also been very involved in training staff within Kelly Marketing Group, as well as speaking at seven conferences on the topic of Establishing Customer Loyalty. I believe the skills I learned as a result of these experiences would be beneficial to XYZ Promotions Ltd. in terms of increasing and maintaining its customer base.

Others would describe me as a self-starter who is determined to assist a company in reaching their goals. I have excellent communication and presentation skills. I am familiar with the advantages and disadvantages of a wide range of media possibilities, a need that you identified in your advertisement. (personal characteristics - CHART C on page 27 + CHART E on page 33)

I believe I am well-qualified for the position you have advertised and could make a meaningful contribution to XYZ Promotions. My resume is enclosed for your consideration. I look forward to hearing from you and would welcome the opportunity to meet you in person to discuss this opportunity.

In your closing paragraph express your interest in having an interview. You may indicate how you will follow-up this letter if you are intending to email or telephone the person you have sent the letter to.

Use a complimentary
closing such as
"Best Regards",
or "Sincerely", or
"Respectfully yours", etc.

Kindest regards,

TYPES OF LETTERS

BROADCAST LETTER

This is a letter sent to companies where no job has been advertised. It could be compared to direct-mail advertising. Response rates are generally low. For better responses, research companies and strive for the name of an actual person you can send the letter to. Include your resume and mention a specific manner in which you will follow-up this letter.

COVER or RESPONSE LETTER

This is a letter that is sent in response to a job advertisement. Include your resume. This is the basic letter outlined on page 66.

NETWORKING LETTER

This is a letter that you send to help establish contacts who can provide advice or assistance to help you in your job search. In following up a networking letter you are hoping to gain the name of someone who may be hiring in the area that you are interested in. Another purpose of a networking letter is to give you the opportunity to talk to someone in a company concerning the type of person they might be hiring if a job was available. It is important in this letter (and in the follow-up) that you ask this person to help you as you seek a job rather than expecting this person to provide a job for you.

THANK YOU LETTER

Thank you letters (and/or Thank You cards) can be sent out to people who have interviewed you for a job, given you advice, or provided contacts to help you find a job. They can also be sent to counselors or career advisors (or teachers, relatives or former employers) who have helped you in some way in your job search. People like to be thanked, and people remember people who thank them.

A strong resume can not only help you to get a job interview but it can provide a structure for the interview.

WRITING A STRONG RESUME

Many job searchers believe their resume is the critical factor to help them get a job. A resume is part of any job application, but it is not the only part. In fact, the resume is really an attempt to help you get a job interview. Based on the reality that most jobs have more than one person applying (and sometimes many more), it is important for you to understand the components of successful resume writing as well as the do's and don'ts of composing a professional looking resume.

Employers often use resumes as a screening device (a necessary part of their jobs based on the number of resumes they receive) to decide who will get an interview. As such, the smallest error (such as a spelling mistake or grammatical error) may result in an application being discarded. When this happens, you do not have the opportunity to defend yourself or correct the mistake. Resumes, along with the cover letter, introduce you to a potential employer. First impressions are important. Similar to any other aspect of job searching, your resume will be more powerful when it is accompanied, where possible, with some form of personal contact.

As with any other aspect of your job search, attempt to get feedback from others regarding your resume. It would be particularly helpful to have people who you may know who are actually involved in hiring for their company give you feedback related to your resume. Counselors/advisors at career centers can also assist you in assessing your resume.

CHAPTER

12

"What one does
is what counts
and
not what one
had the intention
of doing."
Pablo Picasso

In this chapter, you will be given a basic format for writing a resume (there are dozens of sites on the internet to give you many more designs - some internet sites that may be useful to you are listed on the left hand side of this page although this list is by no means comprehensive).

www.workopolis.com
www.monster.com
www.provenresumes.com
www.jobstar.org
www.jobweb.com
www.resume-resource.com

The emphasis in this chapter is to help you to understand the content that makes a positive difference in your resume regardless of the actual format you use. As you write your resume, refer back to work you have done in earlier chapters of this book to help you write a more effective resume. Once you understand the key things to emphasize in your resume, you will be able to adapt this to any format that you decide to use. And remember, match what you are saying to what the job advertisement is asking for.

It is also important to realize that tailoring a resume for a specific job you are applying to will likely be much more successful than preparing one generic resume that you send out by the hundreds. Most successful job seekers have a basic resume that they revise for each job they are applying to.

Although it was suggested on the previous page that you ask some experts (or knowledgeable friends) to help proof and give you feedback on your resume, in the end the best way to evaluate your resume is to ask yourself whether it is working. If you are not getting any job interviews, it may be time to revise your resume.

Pages 71 and 72 provide a sample resume while page 73 provides some tips on writing a more effective resume.

MICHELLE WYSNEWKINSKI

3764 Valleyview Ave   Rochester   NY   14890

Telephone: (555) 787-0934   Email: mwysnewkinski@turbospeed.com

JOB OBJECTIVE

Public Relations Manager

PERSONAL PROFILE

(see CHART D on page 29, CHART E on page 33, CHART H on page 44 and CHART I on page 50)

- B.A. in Media Communications
- received Industry Media Award
- constantly exceeds performance criteria on assignments
- often selected by management to troubleshoot conflict concerns with customers
- self-starter, works well in a fast-paced environment
- more than five years experience Microsoft Office Professional and Adobe Photoshop

ACCOMPLISHMENTS

(see CHART J on page 56)

- as team chairperson helped to increase customer base by 36.3%
- assistant manager of 8 that saw a reduction of 64% in absenteeism over 3 years
- as a member of the company administrative team we exceeded sales goals over a two year period by 18.6%
- presented workshops at 7 conferences over past two years on "Establishing Customer Loyalty"

SKILLS

(see CHARTS B + C on page 27 and CHART D on page 29)

- excellent proficiency with all aspects of Microsoft Office Professional, Adobe Photoshop, Final Cut Pro, and Adobe Illustrator
- strong analytical and listening skills to assist in identifying the needs of customers and to offer positive solutions to customer concerns and perceptions
- excellent presentation skills including the mastery of workshop presentations, video production techniques, and web conferencing
- familiarity with designing needs based surveys, interpreting the data of such surveys, and implementing programs to address the identified needs
- excellent skills in motivating other team members to reach department goals
- excellent communication skills appropriate to a wide range of media possibilities including but not limited to television, radio, internet, and print

MICHELLE WYSNEWKINSKI

Telephone: (555) 787-0934   Email: mwysnewkinski@turbospeed.com

WORK EXPERIENCE

Kelly Marketing Group - Assistant Public Relations Manager   2010 to present

West Coast Media Group - Public Relations   2008 - 2010

OTHER RELATED EXPERIENCE

National Post - Public Relations Internship   2007 - 2008

Brown College - Assistant Advertising Manager (part-time), College newspaper   2005 - 2007

Brown College - Advertising Sales Rep., College newspaper (part-time position)   2004- 2005

EDUCATION/TRAINING

Brown College - B.A., major in Media Communications (Honors Standing)   2004 - 2007

   - top class marks in 3 different senior level communication courses

Central High School - Honors Graduation Diploma   1994 - 1998

ASSOCIATION MEMBERSHIPS

Human Resources Professional Association   2010 to present

Association of Professional Public Relations Managers   2010 to present

   - current Vice-President of local chapter

REFERENCES

(strong school and business references available upon request)

TIPS FOR WRITING A STRONG RESUME

1. Your resume creates a first impression. Use good quality 8 1/2 X 11" white bond paper. Use a laser-quality printer to provide clean, clear copies.

2. Use basic fonts such as Times New Roman or Arial. Use a font size of about 12.

3. Keep your resume to no more than two pages. A crowded resume is difficult to read. Keep your resume simple and inviting. White space can help keep the resume attractive and easy to read.

4. Don't lie on your resume and don't exaggerate. Whatever you write on your resume is often referred to in job interviews. Only write content that you can prove if you are asked about it.

5. Avoid using the word "I". Using point form instead of sentences can help you with this.

6. Don't emphasize skills or previous jobs that you are no longer interested in doing. Your resume should emphasize your skills and accomplishments that relate to the job you are applying for.

7. Don't include your height, weight, age, date of birth, place of birth, marital status, health, ethnicity/race, religion, social security number, or other such personal information.

8. Don't be too wordy. Often, less is more.

9. Target your resume to the position you are applying for. Don't write one that you use over and over again for many different jobs. Match your resume to the job advertisement.

10. Ensure that you have no spelling or grammatical errors.

Good luck occurs when preparation meets opportunity.

SUCCESSFUL JOB INTERVIEWS

For most people, the most feared aspect of job searching is the job interview. One of the best ways to combat job interview stress is through preparation for the interview. The interview is one of the most crucial aspects of your job search as you find yourself potentially just one step away from being hired. You will have worked very hard to reach the actual interview, but this dedication must continue if the end result is to lead to success.

This chapter will help you to better prepare for job interviews. From what to wear, to how to answer those difficult questions, careful preparation can make a positive difference. Through a strong interview you can present yourself as a future valued employee.

This chapter provides an overview of types of interviews, tips on handling interview stress, tips on preparing for a job interview, and finally some of the typical questions you might expect to be asked. For those readers who experience significant stress in an interview, it is important to remember that preparation for an interview can be an effective way to lessen the stress. Preparation can involve writing out answers to potential questions as well as practicing actual interviews with a knowledgeable friend and/or career coach/counselor.

After each interview that you experience it is recommended that you take the time to write down the questions you were asked and consider your answers so that you can learn from this experience.

CHAPTER

13

**"Failure
to prepare
is preparing
to fail."**
Benjamin Franklin

TIPS ON PREPARING FOR A JOB INTERVIEW

1. Ensure you know the time, date and location for your interview. If possible, learn the names and positions of those who will be interviewing you. By driving to the company a few days before your interview you can ensure you know how long it takes to get there as well as viewing what employees are wearing.

2. A key to impressing anyone is being confident. It is easier to be confident when you have prepared answers to potential questions and practiced answering them. Research the company, and also be prepared to talk about what a person does in the position you are applying for.

3. Read and reread your resume and cover letter preparing specific examples from previous job experiences to illustrate the things you have said about yourself.

4. Read the job advertisement several times. Highlight the important aspects of what the company is looking for and think about how you can include this information in your answers to questions.

5. Prepare a list of questions you would like to ask the company.

6. Dress for success. When you feel good about what you are wearing, you will be more confident. Avoid perfumes, excessive jewelry, and avoid smoking immediately before an interview.

7. Have paper, a quality pen, your resume, your questions, any reference letters, or other supporting documents ready the night before.

TIPS ON HANDLING JOB INTERVIEW STRESS

1. It is normal and okay to feel some stress
when you are being interviewed for a job.

2. One of the best ways to reduce stress is
by being well prepared.

3. If you are asked a question that is difficult for you to answer,
attempt to stay calm, positive, smile, and simply do your best.
When you are asked difficult questions the manner in which you
answer may be as important as your actual answer.

4. Make a positive first impression with a firm handshake,
smile, and good posture.

5. Make sure you arrive at least 15 minutes
before the interview. As you are waiting for your interview
be positive with anyone you meet.

6. Use stress reduction strategies such as exercising
or breathing techniques to reduce stress on a
regular basis. Once you have developed stress reduction
habits you can use these techniques to
help you stay more relaxed during an interview.
In addition, remember that you can decide
whether a job interview is a horrible experience
or a wonderful opportunity. It is your choice!

7. Visualize success. In your mind, before the interview,
picture yourself creating a strong positive impression
and effectively answering the questions you are asked.

TIPS FOR DIFFERENT INTERVIEW TYPES

TELEPHONE INTERVIEW: These are sometimes used to screen applicants to decide who will actually get an interview. Keep your answers brief, but always attempt to support what you are saying by giving specific examples. Keep your prepared answers to typical job interview questions handy as a guide for such an interview.

ONE-TO-ONE INTERVIEW: These are traditionally the most common form of interview. Ensure you maintain eye contact with the interviewer and call him/her by name.

GROUP INTERVIEW: Write down the names of the people interviewing you. Focus on the person who has asked you the current question. Make a positive impression on the group one person at a time.

SERIAL INTERVIEW: Sometimes you may be interviewed by several people but not necessarily at the same time. Keep notes on your answers after each interview so you are consistent in your responses.

VIDEO CONFERENCING INTERVIEW: In general, prepare for the interview as though you were in a room with the actual person. Speak clearly. Avoid bright colors. Maintain eye contact with the camera. If this is being conducted over the internet, ensure you are using a dependable computer. In addition, if you will be at home for this interview, consider what is in the room or on the wall behind you that will also show up in the interview. Strive to create a positive impression even with the physical appearance of the room you will be in.

AUDITION INTERVIEW: In this interview you may be asked to demonstrate some of your actual skills. Make sure you understand what you are being asked to do before you begin any task. Remain calm and focused on the task.

MEANDERING INTERVIEW: Occasionally, you might be interviewed by someone who has trouble maintaining a focus in the interview. In such situations, look for opportunities to provide answers to the major questions you were expecting even if they are not asked.

MEAL TIME INTERVIEW: In some situations, you may be required to join an interviewer during lunch or dinner. Often, in such a situation, there is an emphasis on looking at your social skills. Takes cues from your interviewer as to when to sit down, etc. Avoid stories or jokes that present you or anyone else in a bad manner. Explore common interest areas

SAMPLE JOB INTERVIEW QUESTIONS

As you experience job interviews (or talk to others who have been through job interviews), keep a list of your own job interview questions. In addition, explore the internet for other samples of interview questions. The following provide some of the most often used generic questions but they do not include specific questions that might be "skill" or "knowledge" based for specific careers.

1. Tell me about yourself.
2. What do you know about our company?
3. What do you know about the expectations of the job you are applying for?
4. Why should we hire you?
5. Where do you see yourself as being in 5 years?
6. What do other people generally say about you?
7. What would former employers say about you?
8. What would former co-workers say about you?
9. Tell me about a difficult situation you handled well in a former job.
10. Tell me about a significant achievement you made in a former job.
11. Give me an example of a task you had to complete under pressure.
12. Tell me how you handle stress.
13. What kinds of decisions do you find the most difficult to make?
14. Why did you leave your last job?
15. What are your strengths?
16. What are your weaknesses?
17. Why do you want to work here?
18. How do you stay professionally current?
19. How would you best describe your ideal job?
20. What do you think it takes to be successful in this job?
21. Describe a time you worked successfully as part of a team.
22. What motivates you?
23. Give me an example when you used good judgment to solve a problem.
24. Give me an example when you had to work with someone who didn't like you.
25. What would you do if a co-worker was not doing his/her share of the work?

(continued on the next page)

SAMPLE JOB INTERVIEW QUESTIONS

26. What steps would you follow to solve a problem?
27. Describe a time when you were not very satisfied
with your work performance.
28. Have you done this type of work before?
29. What is the salary that you expect?
30. How would you handle a situation with an angry customer or co-worker?
31. What will your references tell us about you?
32. Tell me about a personal challenge you have faced.
33. What specific skills do you have that are required for this job?
34. Tell me a little about a situation
where you had a disagreement with a co-worker.
35. What is the biggest problem you have faced recently
and how did you handle it?
36. What part of this job is least attractive to you?
37. What part of this job appeals to you the most?
38. What are the hours of work you are looking for?
39. What would you like to achieve in this job?
40. Tell me about some of your accomplishments in a former job.
41. How would you describe your most recent job performance?
42. What kind of supervisor do you work best for?
43. How has your education/training helped you prepare for this position?
44. Do you prefer to work alone or as part of a team?
45. What could you do to "fit into" a new work environment?
46. What three personal traits best describe you?
47. What makes a good manager?
48. Why do you want this job?
49. What are some trends that you see in the future for our industry?
50. Describe what you think would be a typical day in this job.

Some thoughts on possible answers to 10 of the most frequently
asked questions are provided on the next two pages.

10 COMMON INTERVIEW QUESTIONS AND ANSWER TIPS

As you answer each of the following, emphasize:

- the positive
- use specific examples to support what you are saying (remember, you have examples from activities throughout this book to support your answers)
- how the company would benefit from hiring you

1. Tell me about yourself . . . (see CHART E on page 33 and CHART H on page 44)
Select 2-3 of your strengths that tie in with what the company is looking for. Be confident, but not arrogant. Stress how your strengths can help the company.

2. What are your strengths/weaknesses? (see CHART E on page 33 and CHART H on page 44)
Your strengths should be answered similar to #1 above. For your weaknesses, be honest, but avoid anything that makes you look bad in your relationship with others. If possible, choose a weakness that you are currently trying to resolve such as "My typing speed is 30 words per minute, but I am taking an evening course in keyboarding to help improve this."

3. Why do you want to work for us?
This is an opportunity to show that you know something about the company. Present a position impression of the company and show how your skills/training are a good match for the company.

4. Why should we hire you? (see CHART J on page 56 and CHART H on page 44)
Talk about what you can do for the company in relationship to their needs.

10 COMMON INTERVIEW QUESTIONS AND ANSWER TIPS

5. Tell me about a conflict you had with a former co-worker or manager and how you handled it. (see CHART G on page 41 and the other tips on page 40)

Choose an example that has a positive resolution if possible. Stress that you handled this in private and attempted to understand the other person.

6. What are your short term/long term goals?

Your short term goal would be to be making a positive contribution to the company as quickly as possible. Hopefully, five years from now you will have greater responsibilities allowing you to take on greater challenges within the company. Stress that you will be loyal to the company.

7. Describe your ideal boss.

Never belittle any former supervisor or manager. Select words such as fair, honest, good listener and optimistic to describe your ideal boss. Also mention that you would like to work with someone who is dedicated to the company and has a vision of where the company is going.

8. Describe a time when you worked on a team project.

Talk about how you believe that a team can be more effective than an individual completing a task. Emphasize cooperation, good listening skills and the need to support others.

9. Tell me about a time when you failed doing something.

Don't try to avoid this question. We all have our failures. Avoid examples that portray you in a bad manner in your relationship with others. Talk about growing and learning from your failures.

10. Describe one of your most important achievements. (see CHART J on page 56)

Be specific. Tell the achievement as a story. Show how your achievement helped the company you worked for. Explain what you did and how others benefited from your accomplishment. Think about a time when you saved the company money or found a better way of doing something. If you are using a non-work example, stress how your achievement made you a better person or helped others.

SOME THOUGHTS ON GOOD LUCK

"Those who succeeded at anything and didn't mention luck
are kidding themselves."
Larry King

"I'm a great believer in luck,
and I find that the harder I work, the more I have of it."
Thomas Jefferson

"Luck is when opportunity knocks and you answer."
Anonymous

"The day you decide to do it is your lucky day."
Japanese Proverb

"Each misfortune you encounter
will carry in it the seed of tomorrow's good luck"
Og Mandino

"Opportunity is missed my most because
it is dressed in overalls and looks like work."
Thomas Edison

"Luck is what happens when preparation meets opportunity."
Seneca

"Our deepest fear is not that we are inadequate.
Our deepest fear is that we are powerful beyond measure."
Marianne Williamson

"The thing that is really hard, and really amazing,
is giving up on being perfect and beginning the work of becoming yourself."
Anna Quindlen

"There are no short cuts to any place worth going."
Beverly Sills

NOTES

NOTES

OTHER BOOKS BY BRIAN HARRIS

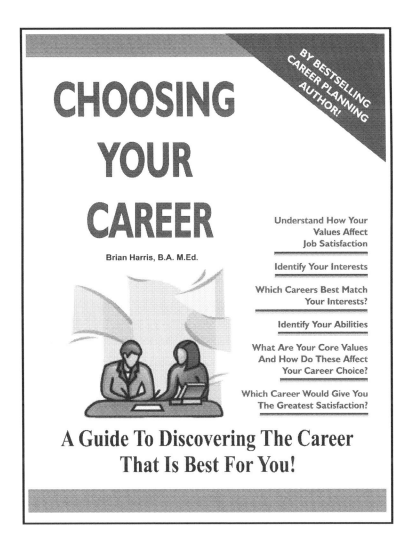

CHOOSING YOUR CAREER
ISBN # 978-1460930885
soft cover - 80 pages

This book, for adults (including college students) includes a self-scoring interest inventory, an informal survey of your skills/abilities and a self-scoring assessment of your values. This can help you identify your strengths and as a result show you which careers are the best match for you.

www.millionairelifeguard.com

OTHER BOOKS BY BRIAN HARRIS

THE MILLIONAIRE LIFEGUARD
ISBN # 9781451509472
soft cover - 174 pages

Two young adults seek the help of a legendary lifeguard in Hawaii. As they attempt to discover his magic formula for financial success, their lives are changed forever as they encounter experiences beyond their control.

www.millionairelifeguard.com

OTHER BOOKS BY BRIAN HARRIS

CHAPTER TITLES

1. What Are Employers Looking For

2. Identifying Your Future Goals

3. Developing A Positive Attitude

4. Identifying Your Skills

5. Developing Effective People Skills

6. Identifying Your Work Ethic

7. The Importance of Being Adaptable

8. Tips For Marketing Yourself

9. Writing Effective Cover Letters

10. Writing A Strong Resume

11. Successful Job Interviews

THE JOB SUCCESS HANDBOOK
By Brian Harris, B.A., M.Ed.
ISBN # 9781460906316 - Soft Cover - 258 pages

THE JOB SUCCESS HANDBOOK provides 201 classroom activities that teachers/career counselors can use with high school students. The activities include black-line masters for handouts that can be freely photocopied for your students. THE JOB SUCCESS HANDBOOK is based on the major factors that employers look for when they hire. In addition to helping your students to get hired into jobs (whether full-time as they leave school, or part-time to help support their future educational costs), these factors can also help your students to be more successful in school.

This book can save teachers hours of preparation time.

www.millionairelifeguard.com